Let Us Talk To God

Deborah L. Lyons

WESTBOW
PRESS
A DIVISION OF THOMAS NELSON
& ZONDERVAN

Good News Translation® (Today's English Version, Second Edition)
Copyright © 1992 American Bible Society. All rights reserved.

WestBow Press books may be ordered through booksellers or by contacting:

WestBow Press
A Division of Thomas Nelson & Zondervan
1663 Liberty Drive
Bloomington, IN 47403
www.westbowpress.com
1 (866) 928-1240

ISBN: 978-1-4908-5330-7 (sc)

Library of Congress Control Number: 2014917186

Printed in the United States of America.

WestBow Press rev. date: 01/14/2015

Contents

Acknowledgments

First Of All, I Thank God For Being The Head Of My Life,
Cause Without Him, I Can Do Nothing,
But With Him, I Can Do All Things,
Father God,
You Are Awesome And Great And You Are
Welcome, In My Life Now And Forever,
I would like to thank Rev. Roger Allen, Keysha Carrington, Kim Carrington,
Czarion Carrington, Stacey Lacks, Damien White, and Charles Jones,
angels whom God sent to be in my life at the most perfect time,
"I love you all, with the love of the lord"

Dedication

I DEBORAH LOUISE CARRINGTON LYONS
WOULD LIKE TO DEDICATE THIS BOOK OF GOD,
TO MY HUSBAND WILLIE LYONS AND MY SON GARY W. CARRINGTON
TO WHOM I PRAY WILL KNOCK, SEEK AND ASK GOD,
TO COME INTO THERE LIFE RIGHT NOW
IN JESUS NAME... AMEN

We Ask for Change

Father in the name of Jesus,

We come to you today,

To confess our sins,

We are enslaved by man made rules,

Let us be set free, right now,

We give up pornography, drugs, and alcohol,

We ask for change in our addictions,

Our attitudes, our ideas, and our focus,

Speak to our issues father God,

Take our weakness and make us solid as a rock,

Help us to shake the devil off,

Every habit is Broken, every chain is broken

Return to us, new lights, new joys, and new beginnings,

We have the victory,

In Jesus name..... Amen

Wonderful Counselor

Wonderful counselor,
Our hearts are full this morning,
With gratitude for all that you have done,
Help us to stay aware of your presence,
And fill us with your holy spirit,
That only you can, transform us in your image,
Father God, right now here in your sanctuary,
We invite you,
To come live inside of us,
Now and forever,
We pray now that your word will be deposited in our hearts,
That we might obey it and receive its benefits,
In the mighty name of Jesus
Amen

Gratitude

Father in Jesus name,

We thank you,

For all that you have already done,

We enter into your gates with thanksgiving and into your courts with praises

Lord, we come before you right now,

Asking for a supernatural move,

Into the lives of these your people,

We pray that there will be,

A turn around concerning finance problems,

A turn around and concerning job recovery,

We come against every spirit,

Of sickness and diseases,

Satan, we break your power and influences,

In the mighty name of Jesus we say,

Amen

Our Bright and Morning Star

Our bright and morning star,

Give us a courageous heart,

When facing trials and Tribulations,

Plant your word in our hearts, and equip our hearts to receive you,

And remove all darkness within us,

Give us; father God, a burning desire

To Read and Study your Word,

Help us to understand and fulfill your will,

Direct our path,

Teach us your ways,

For many are called but, few are chosen,

We thank you for your ever present help, in our times of troubles,

These many blessings and all blessings,

We ask in your holy and righteous name,

We say....amen

Father in Heaven

Father in Heaven
We are not worthy to come to you,
Please, come to us,
Help us to confront our sins,
And help us to keep our eyes on your word,
Because, "the word of God is alive and active,
Sharper than any double edged sword,
It cuts all the way through,
To where soul and spirit meet,
To where joints and marrow come together,
It judges the desires and thoughts of the heart,
Father God, break the chains that have us bound,
Satan we bind you, stay out of our dreams,
Stay out of our lives, you are a liar and you are under our feet,
In the mighty name of Jesus,
We say.... Amen

Master and Creator

Master and creator,

We want our worship to extend beyond our church,

Help us to listen to your promptings,

And to serve other wherever we go,

Father God, how sweet are your words,

They are sweeter than honey,

They give us wisdom knowledge and understanding,

Lord, help us to digest them,

And let them nourish our minds,

Our emotions and our wills,

Please forgive us,

For the times,

When we rush through your word,

Without getting the real meaning or without listening to your soft sweet voice,

Help us Lord to thrive spiritually,

In every way,

In Jesus name, we ask it all

Amen

O Lord My God

O Lord My God,

You have been my defense and refuge in the Day of my Trouble,

When cancer and diseases invade our bodies,

It seems that suddenly we're thrown into a battle bigger than anything

We'll ever have to face, but Father God, you promised to bring something good,

Out of even our darkest moments, even in the worst of times,

Father God we have much to thankful for,

Because we are comforted by the one, who knows all about our sufferings,

Father God, Remove destructive thinking when trails come our way,

Give us strength for today and a bright hope for tomorrow,

As we count our Many Blessings, we see what God has done,

We don't need more to be thankful for; we just need to be more thankful,

May God our father and the Lord Jesus Christ give us grace and peace,

In Jesus Name, Amen

Most Gracious and All Powerful God

Most Gracious and all powerful God,

Help us to enter into a season of favor,

We welcome you into our lives,

Come, come holy spirit, bring us closer to God,

Help us to stop living emotionally,

And live on purpose, help us to put you first,

Your kind and wonderful love, heals our souls, minds, and bodies,

No one can separate us from the love of God,

We know, you will work things out for our good,

Help us remember that we are more than a conqueror,

To him that love us,

And help us to speak boldly for you,

In the mighty name of Jesus, we say... Amen

Almighty God

Almighty God,

Abide in us and we in you,

We want to know you,

In all your fullness,

And love you completely,

Jesus you are the one true leader of us all,

You know what we need and you know where we are the most
vulnerable,

Give us the strength to make you known to others,

Change our hearts,

Fill them with love,

Help us to serve you with a whole heart,

For we can do nothing without you, but with you,

We can do all things through Christ,

That strengthens us,

In Jesus name..... Amen

Nobody Told Us It Would Be Easy

Father in Heaven,

How good it is to give thanks to you O Lord,

Nobody told us it would be easy,

But we don't believe you brought us this far, to leave us,

Father God, we thank you for this day,

We thank you for being able to see and hear the beauty of your creations,

We thank you for your blessings in our lives,

Give us the strength to help the nonbelievers,

Keep us uplifted so that we can encourage others,

We realize that our lives are not our own,

Use us Jesus,

To do your will,

In the name of Jesus we pray.... amen

Father, Who are in Heaven

Father who are in heaven,

How wonderful it is to put aside all of our cares,

And come to you in prayer,

We thank you for sacrificing your life, for our sins,

Because you died and rose again,

We have assurance that one day we'll be with you,

In a Place of no more death,

O heavenly father, we pray,

That you will also fulfill the spiritual needs,

Of each of us, in our families,

We will be ever faithful and ever thankful for our blessings from you,

In the mighty name of Jesus, we say Amen

Teach Us to Do Your Will

Father in Heaven,

Teach us to do your will,

For you are our God,

Your spirit is good,

Lead us into the land of uprightness,

Help us to obey you,

Rather than man,

You are a sun and shield,

You have given us grace and glory,

You said in your word,

"No good thing will be withhold from those who walk uprightly"

We thank you Jesus,

For all that you have done and all that you are still doing,

In the mighty name of Jesus, we say.....Amen

Blessed Savior

Blessed Savior,

We owed a debt, we could not pay,

And Jesus paid a debt, he did not owe,

We thank you father God,

If we had ten thousand tongues,

It would not be enough,

Help us to trust your son as our savior,

And as the Lord who can bring us to you,

Your son died in our place,

And we believe his resurrected life impacts and changes us,

In ways far beyond our ability to understand,

Give us the Grace to realize that change does not take you by surprise,

But is a means, by which you help us to find in you,

Through your son and your spirit,

More than our hearts ever imagined possible,

Amen

Help Us Not to Judge Others

Father in Heaven,

Help us not to judge others,

So that you will not judge us,

And help us to forgive others,

So that you will forgive us,

Give us strength to love our enemies,

And do Good to those who hate us,

And help us to pray for those who mistreat us,

And help us to give to everyone who ask us for something,

And when someone takes what is ours,

Give us the strength to not ask for it back,

Father God, help us to do for others just what we want them to do for us,

Amen

Every Giant

Most gracious and all powerful God,
Every Giant that we are facing right now,
God, is going to slay in the mighty name of Jesus,
And if we ask him,
"God is able to do exceedingly, abundantly, above all that we could ask or think,
According to the power that works in us"
Father God, you know the needs of all or hearts,
Give us new hopes, new strengths
Help us to fly higher than any mountain or any storm,
Father God, you are greater than any battle that we could ever face,
And we thank you that no weapon formed against us shall prosper,
We call it done
In the mighty name of Jesus the Christ... Amen

Blessed Redeemer

Blessed redeemer,

We thank you,

We have been redeemed,

We have been set free,

Those who wait on the Lord,

Shall renew their strength,

They shall mount up with wings like eagles,

They shall run and not be weary,

They shall walk and not faint,

Father, we can do nothing without you,

But with you we can do all things through Christ who strengthens us,

Bless us, Father God, Be gracious unto us,

Keep us an make your face to shine upon us,

Give us peace,

Peace that surpass all understanding,

We stand in confidence,

On the fact, that if God is for us,

Nothing can stand against us,

In Jesus name we say... Praise the Lord Hallelujah Jesus... Amen

We Thank You for Your Word

Blessed savior,

We thank you for your word today,

And we thank you,

That it will not return to you void,

We ask for your renewed strength and courage in serving you,

For our own righteousness is of filthy rags,

We thank you, that we are new creatures in Christ Jesus,

Because of your death,

Sin has no government over our lives,

And we thank you father God,

For when trouble comes,

We already know,

We got the victory,

In Jesus name.... Amen

Spirit of the Living God

Spirit of the living God,
We pray for every person,
Lord, you see those who are sick, suffering, and oppressed,
Now Lord, in you authority,
We speak in Jesus name,
For all disease to depart,
Arthritis, cancer, diabetes, high blood pressure,
Heart trouble, blindness, deafness, and depression,
Loose your hold, the power of sickness is broken,
We receive it right now, in Jesus name,
We repent, of our sins,
Jesus is our Lord, you died for our sins,
We ask you to live inside of us,
And take over our lives, now and forever more
In the mighty name of Jesus... Amen

Lord of Heaven and Earth

Father, Lord of Heaven and earth,

We thank you for giving us your word,

May your holy spirit fill us with confidence,

So we will be able to speak boldly to everyone about your word,

And may the holy spirit direct us in our prayers,

Our actions and our thoughts towards others,

We thank you for giving your only begotten son,

Jesus the Christ,

To die for our sins,

And we thank you for allowing us to serve you,

In Jesus name we pray.... Amen

Everlasting God

Most Gracious and all powerful God,
We claim complete cleansing from sins today,
Through the word of God and by faith in the blood of the lamb,
We are set free from sins,
Father God, you are worthy to receive glory, honor and praise,
For you have created all things and with all our hearts,
We call to you,
Give us wisdom, knowledge, understanding and insight,
Father you are our light and our salvation,
And we shall not fear no evil,
For thou art with us,
Thy Rod an thy staff they comfort us,
Thou preparest a table before us,
In the presence of our enemies,
Thou anointest our head with oil,
Our cup runneth over,
Surely goodness and mercy shall follow us all the days of our lives,
And we shall dwell in the house of the lord forever... Amen

We Claim Complete Cleaning

Father God,

We thank you for your peace that surpass all understanding,

We thank you for peace on our jobs,

Peace at night,

We thank you for providing us with a home where we may always live,

In peace and contentment,

We thank you for letting us know that you are near,

To send us help and guidance,

When we lose our way,

Lord widen our world,

We want to be a part of the work you are doing,

Give us eyes to see as you see,

And Hands to serve others,

And a heart to share your Gospel,

In the mighty name of Jesus we say.... Amen

Open Our Eyes

Most holy and everlasting God,

It seems that sometimes,

We are our own worst enemies,

Lead us today Lord,

As you see fit,

Allow us to demonstrate our faith by encouraging others,

Help us not to keep resentment and bitterness in our hearts,

And to wait patiently for you to work in our lives,

Through the power of the Holy Spirit,

"Help us to let go and let God have his way"

In Jesus name.

Amen

Give Us Faith

Father in the Name of Jesus,

Give us faith of a little child,

Help us to be what you want us to be,

In character, action and will,

Show us you ways, o Lord,

Teach us your path,

Guide us in your truth,

We know that we cannot hide our sins from you,

For you know what's in our hearts,

Father God, we confess them now to you,

We repent our sins,

We love you,

We need you,

We can't do anything on our own,

We believe you died for us,

We receive you in our hearts today,

Amen

We Owed a Debt

Spirit of the living God,
We owed a debt we could not pay,
And Jesus paid a Debt he did not owe,
We thank you,
For giving your only begotten son,
Jesus Christ to die for our sins,
We thank you, father God,
That our hurts and pains matter to you,
We thank you that we are,
The head and not the tail,
Above and not beneath,
Father, you have given us our very breath,
And blessings on top of blessings,
God has supplied our every need,
Surly goodness and mercy,
Shall follow us all the days of our lives,
And we will dwell in the house of the Lord,
Forever...... Amen

We Have Disappointed You

Father, in the name of Jesus,
We are a sinner,
And we know we have disappointed you,
But we're asking for your grace,
Come into our hearts today,
Be our Lord and savior,
Empower us to serve you the rest of our lives,
And give you glory and honor and praise,
Thank you Jesus for saving us,
Thank you Lord for forgiving our sins,
And thank you,
For shredding your blood for us,
In the mighty name of Jesus we say,
Amen

Open Our Eyes

Wonderful counselor,

From whom all blessings flow,

Open our eyes Lord,

To people around us,

Help us to see them as you do,

And to meet others needs,

We thank you that our hurts and pains matters to you,

Draw us near to you Lord,

You are so awesome and great,

You have done so much for us,

Give us the courage to trust and to follow you in your ways,

Amen

The Way, The Truth, and The Light

Father, in the holy name of Jesus,

We come thanking you,

This morning because you have shown us the way,

The truth and the light,

We thank you father God because you have given us all things,

In life, we have said some things that we should not have said,

We have did some things that we should not have done,

We ask for your forgiveness for everything we have done,

Said or thought in contrary to your will,

Please protect us from all dangers and support us with

Your wisdom to accept all things that come our way,

In Jesus name

Amen

We Extol Your Name

Spirit of living God,
We take this time right now to extol your name,
We magnify your name,
Cause you are worthy to receive glory and honor,
For you have created all things,
Father God, use us as an earthly vessel for your word,
Create in us, a life that reflects and glorify you,
Cause greater is he that is in us, than he that's in the world,
Help us father, not to be controlled by human nature,
But live as the spirit tells us to even though,
We walk through the valley of the shadows of death,
We well feel no evil,
Cause God will never leave us alone,
In Jesus name we pray
Amen

We Curse Every Work of Satan

Father in the name of Jesus,
We thank you, because,
You are greater than any,
Enemy or adversary, that we face today,
You are able to restore all those, who are broken,
By your strife,
All sick bodies are healed,
All broken bodies are mended,
We thank you, Lord,
For financial prosperity,
For all who need it,
We ask you father God,
To order our steps, right now,
Direct our lives,
We curse every work of Satan,
His plans, his plots, his tactics,
In the mighty name of Jesus
Amen

Strength to Face Opposition

Almighty God,

Give us strength to face opposition when we stand for you,

Father let us eat the scroll,

So that we may know your words backwards and forwards,

For we know that your words are as sweet as honey,

Help us to stand firm in understanding who you are,

Make us firm in understanding who you are,

Make us firm as a rock and as hard as a diamond,

We are determined to know you,

And your power,

We thank you,

That our residency is in Heaven,

In the mighty name of Jesus,

We say... Amen

Lead Us Not Into Temptation

Father in heaven,

Lead us not into temptation,

But Deliver us from Evil,

We thank you father God,

That trouble don't last always,

We thank you for letting us come in your house,

And not going out the same way we came in,

Help us to want to give to those who need it,

And help us to admit we are sinners,

Come into our hearts right now,

We surrender all,

In the mighty name of Jesus.... Amen

When Trouble Surrounds Us

Holy Spirit,

When trouble surrounds us and we feel so all alone,

Father God say's to call on him,

In the morning, noonday or late at night,

There is no one he can't save,

There's nothing he can't do,

We thank you because you are more than enough,

Touch our families and friends,

Where they hurt the most,

Lift up their spirits father God,

We thank you because you did not leave us to bare our burdens alone,

Amen

We Boldly Proclaim You

Father in Heaven,

Help us to be diligent to present ourselves approved,

By Gods workers who do not need to be ashamed,

Help us to grow in our understanding of your word,

Father God we are thankful,

For your protection on every side,

We are human and we are going to make mistakes sometimes,

Help us to remember that,

We have an obligation,

To diligently seek your truth,

Then we may boldly proclaim you,

Praying that your spirit will guard not only our hearts,

But also the hearts of those we seek to serve God,

For God and his word are deserving,

Of the highest praise, hallelujah Jesus,

These blessings and all blessings,

We ask in your holy and righteous name,

Amen

Storms that Strengthen Us

Spirit of the living God,
Let our Christian lives,
Be a living sermon to all unbelievers,
The very storms that threaten to destroy us,
God, will use to strengthen us,
Jesus death, forgave our past sins,
Let it inspire our present obedience,
And give us hope,
That has its foundation in God,
And let our lives as well as our lips,
Speak for you father God,
In all circumstances, we can give thanks,
That God has not left us to bare our burdens alone,
If we hold on, to God's Truth,
We won't be trapped by Satan's lies,
In Jesus wonderful and unchanging hand,
We ask it all
Amen

Our Rose of Sharon

Our Rose of Sharon,

We give you our burdens right now,

And we thank you,

That when we come to you,

There is no waiting line,

For there is no unimportant people in the body of Christ,

All are equal,

We thank you father God,

Because we all descended from our first parents,

Adam and Eve,

No race, nor ethnicity is superior or inferior to another,

Father, you made us and you gave to all life and breath,

Give us all we need,

So we can give to others in their needs,

In Jesus Name,

We together praise and honor your holy and righteous name

Amen

Blessings Upon Blessings

Father, you said in Romans 10:13

For whosoever shall call upon the Lord shall be saved,

And we know that all things work together,

For the good to them that Love God,

We thank you for lips to speak,

For ears to hear,

For eyes to see,

We thank you for the use of our limbs,

We thank you father God, for you have given us our very breath,

And blessings upon blessings,

In the mighty name of Jesus,

We say........Amen

Walk By Faith and Not By Sight

Father God,

Your word is a lamp unto our feet,

And a light unto our path,

Help us to meditate on your Word,

An then apply it to our daily lives,

And may the mind of Christ our savior,

Live in us from day to day,

Father God, does not want anyone to perish,

But have everlasting life,

His offer of salvation is open to anyone,

Help us father god,

To receive Jesus as savior,

Time after time God stands,

At our door and knock,

Help us to let you in,

And stay connected,

Deliver us out of doubt,

Deliver us out of fear,

Help us to walk and talk by faith and not by sight,

In the might name of Jesus,

We say........ Amen

Satan is A Liar

Heavenly father,
People see what we do,
But God sees why we do it,
We thank you lord,
For giving each of us different talents,
And spiritual gifts,
To be used for your glory,
Help us not to lift up ourselves,
Or think more highly of ourselves, than we should,
Father, your work here on earth is done through us,
Your children,
Help us to keep our eyes on your word,
And be not concerned with what others think,
And to know Satan is a liar,
And he is under our feet,
Show us how to communicate with you father god,
Help us to know, that we know, that we know,
That the word of God, Works,
These many blessings and all blessings,
We ask, in the name of Jesus
Amen

Come Lord

Come, Lord and give us courage,
Make us over comers,
And give us true strengths and power,
That only comes from you to our souls,
Help us to stand fast in the faith,
And be brave and be strong,
Father God, reach out to us and pull us out of our pit,
You have the key,
When you open a door no one can close it,
And when you close it, no one can open it,
Help us father God, to trust you,
For we don't even know what our life tomorrow will be,
We are like a puff of smoke,
Which appears for a moment and disappears,
Help us to walk hand and hand with you forever,
Amen

Holy Spirit, All Divine

Holy Spirit, all divine,

Speak to us Lord,

In all Three of your Ways,

In a Soft Voice,

In a dream,

An through vision,

Lift up our Spirits,

And Renew Us Today,

Help us to pour our Hearts out to you father God

Search us,

You know if there are wicked ways in us,

Cleanse us from every wrong thought or ways,

Be merciful to us,

We are sinners an we are sorry,

We trust and love you,

We take you as our lord and savior,

We give your name glory and honor,

We magnify your name,

We ask for eternal life,

That you have already paid for with your blood,

We ask it all

In the name of Jesus.....Amen

We Stand Amazed

Father God,

We stand amazed and at Awe,

At how much you love and care for us,

Because we realize,

We are nothing without you,

We're not worthy of anything,

Our life on this earth is but a moment,

Like a puff of smoke,

Which appears then disappears,

Help us to be quick to listen,

And slow to speak,

And slow to become angry,

Father God, help us to get rid of every filthy Habit,

Help us to submit to you Lord,

The word that you plant in our hearts,

Which is able to save us,

Thanks be to God,

Which gives us the victory,

In the mighty name of Jesus

Amen

Wait on the Lord

Wait on the Lord from day to day,

For God so loved the world,

That he gave his only begotten son,

That whosoever believeth in him shall not perish,

But have everlasting life,

Father God, as we read your prophetic word,

Help our faith to be stimulated and strengthened,

So that your spirit can be infused in a divine manner,

Father God, there is a greater purpose in our life,

Than we have yet discovered,

Father, let no mystery be withheld from our minds,

By your spirit father God,

Open our minds and our hearts.

Even now, as we face decisions, let your spirit work,

Instilling in us a new,

Greater understanding in the way we should go,

May God our father and the lord Jesus Christ,

Give us grace and peace,

In the name of Jesus... Amen

In the Beginning

In the beginning, the word already existed,

The word was with God,

And the word was God,

The word became a human being,

And full of grace and truth,

Out of the fullness of your grace, father God,

You have blessed us all, giving us blessings after another,

Help us to be aware that we do not forget you Lord,

Because of all the material things that you have given us,

We sometimes focus on ourselves and the gifts,

And not on the giver,

Help us to remember that we rather have Jesus,

Than silver and gold,

Give us faith,

For without faith, It is impossible to please you,

For he who comes to God,

Must believe that he is,

And that he is a rewarder of those who diligently seek him,

We ask in Jesus name...

Amen

Wonderful Example

We thank you father God,

That you know our hearts,

With our pains and our joys,

Let nothing be done through selfish ambition or conceit,

Help us to look out not only for our own interests,

But also for the interest of others,

In this world father God,

We know we will have trials and tribulations,

Hold us close during our trails,

And to help us to be of good cheer,

Give us the strength we need over come,

Help us to seek righteousness,

As we focus on Jesus wonderful example,

In Jesus name..

Amen

We're Thankful Lord

We're thankful Lord,
That our achievements, success or greatness,
Are not rooted in ourselves,
But are the product of Gods, Grace,
Which we are eternally dependent,
We thank you father God,
You said in your word,
"God resists the proud, but gives grace to the humble"
We thank you,
That this hope does not disappoint us,
We thank you,
That God has poured out his love into our hearts,
By means of the holy spirit,
And we thank you for our gifts from you,
Each and every day,
Lord, you alone deserve thanks and praises
And May God our father and the Lord Jesus Christ,
Give us grace and peace
In Jesus Name..... Amen

Behold

Behold the Lord's hand is not shortened,

That it cannot save,

Nor his ears heavy,

That it cannot hear,

For our life is a winding road,

With unknown troubles,

Help us Lord,

To stand firm,

When it seems,

We can't change directions,

Help us to be steadfast in our walk with you,

Immovable,

Always abounding in the work of the Lord,

Knowing that our labor is not in vain,

And help us to be followers of peace,

Not of anger,

We thank you,

For continuing to help us and walking with us,

We can be certain father God,

That you are right beside us,

Securely leading and guiding us,

In the name of Jesus..... Amen

The Earth is the Lord's

The earth is the Lord's and all its fullness,

Jesus said in his word:

"I am the bread of life,

He who comes to me shall never hunger,

And he who believes in me shall never thirst",

Father God, there is nothing in this universe,

More worthy of our enthusiasm than,

Who Christ is,

And what he did for us,

Fill our hearts with the joy of Christ,

We desire that the abundant life we have found in you,

Might reach out to others around us,

Help us to celebrate,

In knowing you,

You came so that we may have life,

And that we may have it more abundantly,

In all circumstances father God,

We can give thanks, that you have not left us on our own,

In Jesus name,

Amen

God Made Us Plain and Simple

Ecclesiasts 7:29 says,

God made us plain and simple,

But we have made ourselves very complicated,

Lord, give us the grace to face,

All challenges in our lives,

We thank you,

For the life that you have given us,

We are satisfied with what we have,

And in the mist of our battles,

Help us to remember we are more than a conqueror,

Through him that love us,

Father God, we break the chains right now of,

Sickness,

Depression,

Fear and envy

These blessings and all blessings,

We ask in your righteous and holy name,

Amen

A Sincere Prayer

Father in Heaven,
There have been times in our lives,
So many trails, tribulations on every side,
But we know a man,
They call him Jesus,
He has opened up our eyes,
And showed us how to walk,
He gave us his book of life,
And told us, he's always by our side,
He'll never leave us nor forsake us,
Father God, when we get on our knees,
And say a sincere prayer,
We'll find that there's power in the name of Jesus,
And we're asking you Jesus,
To cover us with your blood,
In the mighty name of Jesus,
Amen

Now to Him, Who is Able

Now to him, who is able, to do exceedingly,

Abundantly above all that we ask,

Or think according to the power that works in us,

We thank you for demonstrating your own love to ward us,

In that while we were still sinners, you died for us,

Father God, we're far from perfection,

We thank you for equipping us with your inspired word,

You have given us the tool we need to live for you,

Help us to take the time to read it

And to follow what it say's to do,

In the name of Jesus we say

Amen

Blessed

Blessed is the man who walks not in the counsel of the ungodly,

Nor stand in the path of sinners,

Bless the Lord o my Lord,

And forget not all his benefits,

Who forgives all our iniquities,

Who heals all diseases,

Who redeem our life from destruction,

Who crowns us with loving kindness and tender mercies,

We thank you for boundaries,

We thank you for being a fence around us,

We thank you for being an awesome God,

And may the God of all grace,

Who called us to his eternal glory,

By Christ Jesus,

After we have suffered a while,

Perfect, establish, strengthen, and settle us,

In the mighty name of Jesus,

Amen

O Lord, Our Lord,

We claim complete cleansing from sins today,
Through the word of God,
And by faith in the Blood of the Lamb,
We are set free from sins,
We call to you,
The most high God who supply's our every need,
We're not worthy of anything father God,
But you are worthy to be praised,
You are worthy to receive glory, honor and power,
For you have created all things,
An by your will they were given existence and life,
Show us our ways, O Lord
Teach us your Paths,
Guide us in your truth,
For you are our God and savior,
In the mighty name of Jesus,
We say..... Amen

He Knows All About Us

Father in heaven, who knows all about us,

We offer our day to you,

Lift up our hearts to heaven,

There is a loving and kind father there,

Who offers release comfort and peace,

We're not worthy of what you have done for us and yet now,

You are doing even more,

Father, there is none like you,

You are God all by yourself,

We ask you to inspire our thoughts,

Guide our actions,

And may our lives and words show your loving grace,

In the mighty name of Jesus we say,

Amen

Pray for Every Soul

Lord of heaven and earth,
We pray for every soul to be saved today,
We believe you have given us the power,
To bless people and we're asking for a blessing,
Upon our lives and we're asking it in your name Jesus!
We thank you father God, that whatever
You bless cannot be cursed,
Bless us in everything we do,
Everywhere we go and bless every word that comes out our mouth,
Let them be pleasing to you Jesus,
We thank you for opening up right doors and closing wrong doors,
We bless the Lord at all times,
And his praises shall continually be in our mouth,
In the name of Jesus we say,
Amen

Fill Us with Your Holy Spirit

Father in the mighty name of Jesus,

Fill us with your holy spirit,

That only you can,

Use us to do your will,

You said in your word:

Anyone who is not for me, is really against me and anyone,

Who does not help me gather is really scattering,

Father God, here we are in the name of Jesus,

Help us,

For you are the potter and we are the clay,

Mold us into what you will have us to be,

We Repent of our sins,

We love you, we need you,

We believe you died for us,

We receive you in our hearts right now,

In Jesus name,

Amen

Touch Each and Everyone

Spirit of the living God,

Go into the homes,

Of all the people that's sick,

Suffering, that cries out in pain,

Touch each and every one with a finger of love,

Touch the one that's being mistreated and misunderstood,

And go into the old folks homes, prisons, hospital, the air force,

Army, navy, marines, wrap your loving arms around them father God,

Keep them safe from all hurt, harm and dangers,

Father God we stretch our arms out to you,

With no other help we know,

We just want to thank you for being God all by yourself,

Thank you father God for sitting up high and looking down low,

For we realize that our life is not our own,

Use us Jesus to do your will each day,

We give your name all honor, Praise and glory,

Hallelujah Jesus and we know that we're not worthy of anything,

But we thank you for loving us,

Amen

Remove All Impurities

Spirit of the living God,
Let the words of our mouth and the meditation of our hearts,
Be acceptable in your sight,
O lord forgive us Father God,
For the times our speech crosses the line,
And forgive us when our speech hurt others,
Remove all impurities and then start us a new,
With strength and courage,
You said in your word:
Your strength is made perfect in weakness,
Father we are totally dependent on you,
Let your spirit work in us,
Give us a greater control over our present and future plans,
And as we come closer to you father God, let us feel,
That inner power growing with new boldness,
And help us to walk by faith and not by sight,
In Jesus wonderful name we ask it all,
Amen

Bless Us Today

Dear Jesus, we pray that you will bless us today,

Spiritually, physically and financially,

And please dear Lord, help us to make good decisions in this life,

And give us the desires of our hearts,

"Evening and morning and at noon, we will pray and he shall hear our voices"

Let us be obedient to Gods instructions,

So your spirit will create in us awareness of which steps to take and which steps not to take,

We ask you lord, to direct our steps and paths,

Lead us away from those who would damage the plans of God for us,

And take us toward the path that leads to that fulfillment we seek,

We thank you and ask you in your holy and righteous name we say,

Amen

Keep Us from Stumbling

To him, who is able to keep us from stumbling,
Father God, praise your holy and righteous name, if God is for us,
Who can be against us,
We are persuaded that neither death, nor life,
Nor angels, nor principalities, nor powers, nor things presents,
Nor things to come, nor, any other created things,
Shall be able to separate us from the love of God
Satan your lies and your weapons will not prosper,
Because, we are fearfully and wonderfully made,
And we "are children of the most high God"
We are the righteousness of God" and you said in your word,
You will give us "beauty for ashes"
In the mighty name of Jesus, we say
Amen

How We Love to Call Your Name

Father in Heaven,

How we love to call your name,

Jehovah Jireh, Jehovah shalom, the way,

The truth and the light,

We are children of the highest God, we are the righteousness of God,

And we thank you for removing our sins as far as the east is from the west,

We thank you for remembering that we are dust,

We know that we are not worthy of anything,

But we thank you for loving us, we thank you for lifting us up,

We thank you for letting us see one more day,

These many blessings and all we ask in your holy and righteous name,

And we say

Amen

If I be Lifted Up

Jesus said "if I be lifted up,

I'll draw all men unto me." Father God,

Let the words of my mouth and the meditation of my heart

Be acceptable in your sight, O Lord

Bless the Lord, O my soul,

And forget not,

All his benefits,

Who forgive all our iniquities,

Who heals all our diseases,

Who redeem our lives from destruction,

Who crowns us with loving kindness and tender mercies,

We thank you father God, we are not here for misery,

But to enjoy our lives

Help us to be pure in our heart,

Help us trust in you Lord,

With all our hearts and you shall direct our paths,

And may the God of hope,

Fill us with all joy and peace,

In believing that we may abound in hope, by the power the Holy Spirit

We ask it all, in Jesus name

Amen

All Powerful God

Most holy and all powerful God,

Guide us from heaven now,

You know all things,

Bless our homes father God,

Let it become a pleasant place,

That is just filled with your loving presence and peace,

Help us to respond to your love for us by loving others in return,

Teach us to do your will,

For you are our God,

Our leader and our guide,

These many blessings and all blessings we

Ask in your holy and righteous name

Amen

means of our faith The Source of Hope

Blessed savior,

May God,

The source of hope,

Fill us with all joy and peace,

By means of our faith in him,

So that our hope will continue to grow by the power of the Holy Spirit,

Father God, fill our minds with those things that are good,

That deserves praises,

Things that are true, noble, pure and honorable,

Help us put into practice your words and your actions,

In the name of Jesus

Amen

Our Hearts are Full

Father in heaven,

Our hearts are filled with wonderful happiness because you have sent

your only begotten son,

Jesus the Christ to be with us all the days of our lives,

No longer are we lonely,

No longer are we lost,

Thank you father God for all you have done,

Seen and unseen,

Look down from heaven upon us,

Father and bless us,

Give your angels charge over us,

In all our ways so that our lives may be a thing of lasting beauty and joy,

Pleasing always in your sight,

We love you, be our Lord and savoir

Amen

Let Us Give Thanks

Let us give thanks to the God and father of our Lord Jesus Christ,

The merciful father,

The God from whom all our help comes from,

Father you said in your word:

"Fix our attention, not on things that are seen,

For they last only for a time,

But on what cannot be seen lasts forever",

We know that when this tent we live in here on earth is torn down,

You will have a house in heaven for us to live in,

A home you yourself has made,

Which will last forever,

We thank you Lord for giving us your inspired words,

They are all the tools we need to live for you,

Help us father God to take time to read,

Them and follow what you tell us to do,

In Jesus name we say,

Amen

The Head and Not the Tail

Father, in the name of Jesus,
Help us to know who we are,
And to love ourselves when life pulls us down,
You said in your words,
"We are the head and not the tail,
Above and not beneath"
Then you said:
"I will give you double for your troubles"
If we stand on Your Word,
So no matter what we go through,
No Matter what we have gone through,
We realize that the battle is not ours,
It belongs to you,
Our life in not our own,
Use us to do your will each day,
We Surrender all to you father God,
In the mighty name of Jesus
Amen

A Bridge over Trouble Water

Most gracious and all powerful God,

We thank you for your son Jesus Christ,

He's a mighty good leader.

He's a bridge over trouble water,

He was born to die,

And saved the whole world,

Hallelujah Jesus,

When we get sick,

You heal us,

When we have problems,

You is a problem solver,

You gave us a new way of walking,

You gave us a new way of talking,

You gave us a new way of thinking,

You have opened our eyes,

Now we can see,

We repent of our sins,

We love you, we need you,

We believe you died for us,

We receive you in our hearts right now,

We thank you for everything you have done and

everything you are still doing

Amen

Our Life is Not Our Own

Father, you said in your word:
"You shall love the Lord your God,
With all your heart,
With all your soul,
With all your mind and with all your strength"
We realize this morning that our life is not our own,
You have bought us at a price,
And we magnify your name,
We thank you for everything that you already done
And yet now you are doing even more
We thank you in the name of the father,
The son and the Holy Spirit we say
Amen

Be Content with What We Have

Father in Jesus name, you are so good,
You have provided all we need and so much more,
Help us to be content, with what we have,
Knowing that with out you, we would have neither life nor breath,
Teach us who we are,
So we can be happy being ourselves,
Help us to rejoice in you Lord,
Not just when everything is going good,
Help us to remember it's not what we're going through!
It's where we're going to,
In the mighty name of Jesus,
Amen

Every Time we Turn Around

Father in heaven, who knows all about us,

We just want to say thank you,

It was your blood that saved us,

Every time we turn around, somebody is sick,

Somebody is gone to the hospital,

Somebody have passed and gone on,

Father God, you have brought us through trials and tribulations,

Dangers seen and unseen,

We thank you for everybody you have given us to be in our lives,

We thank you for the time we've had with the ones you have taken back,

Lead us and guide us to do your will and give us strength,

To deal with whatever or whoever we'll,

Have to deal with in order to serve you,

We extol your name Jesus, these many blessing,

And all blessings we ask in your holy name,

Amen

Jesus Birth, Life and Death

Let us give thanks to the God and father of our Lord Jesus Christ:

Jesus Birth, Life and Death,

Paid the Penalties for our sins,

We ask you,

For the strength to bless those who persecute us,

And let us be happy with those who are happy,

And weep with those who weep,

Help us to do everything possible,

To live in peace with everyone,

And Lord whether or not we're able to worship in a beautiful place,

We ask you to create in us beautiful hearts,

That honors you in our times of worship,

Because you are deserving of all praises,

In the name of Jesus.... Amen

Those Who Wait on the Lord

Those who wait on the Lord shall renew their strength,
They shall mount up with wings like eagles,
They shall run and not be weary,
They shall walk and not faint,
Father God, we can do nothing without you,
But with you, we can do all things through Christ, who strengthens us,
We pray for everyone to be saved today,
I believe you have given us the power to bless people,
And we're asking for a blessing upon our lives,
And we're asking it in your name "Jesus",
We thank you father that whatever you bless cannot be cursed,
Bless us in everything we do,
Bless everywhere we go,
Bless every word that comes out of our mouths,
Let them be pleasing to you Lord,
We thank you father God for opening up doors and closing wrong doors,
In the might name of Jesus
Amen

Be Acceptable to God

Everlasting father,
Let the words of our mouth and the meditation of our hearts,
Be acceptable in your sight, O lord,
Our hope is built on nothing less than Jesus,
Blood and righteousness,
We pray that you will look upon our families with,
Understanding and mercy,
We ask you to fulfill all our hopes,
All our dreams and all our needs in this life,
Help us father God, to please you,
Help us to give you, first place in our hearts,
Help us to give you first place in our service,
Whatever we do, Lord, in word or deed,
Let us all do, in the name of Jesus,
Amen

Satan Hates a Confident Person

Father God, we know that Satan hates,

A confident person,

We thank you for authority and power over the enemy,

And if we trust and ask you,

You are able to do exceedingly abundantly above all that we ask or think,

According to the power that works in us, now to him,

Who is able to keep us from stumbling,

We repent of our sins, we love you,

We need you,

We believe you died for us,

We receive you in our hearts right now,

We thank you,

For all that you have done,

And all you are still doing in the mighty name of Jesus,

Amen

Stop Acting Like the World

Jesus, the Christ,
In this world we live in, things are going to go wrong,
We gone read and hear about constant deaths, murders,
Tragic accidents and suicides,
But father God said in his word:
I'll be a father to the fatherless,
A mother to the motherless, a brother to the brotherless,
And a sister to the sisterless,
Nothing can separate us from the love of God,
God wants to give us the desires of our hearts,
He said: we have not because we ask not,
Help us father God to stop acting like the world,
Stop thinking like the world,
We're in this world, but not of this world,
And help us to call things,
Be not as though they were, in Jesus name
Amen

Jehovah Jireh

Jehovah Jireh,

We come to you this morning, not asking for anything,

But we come to you with a heart full of thanks,

Thanking you that you said in your word:

"Where two or three are gathered together in your name,

There you are also in the mist of them,

We thank you for showing us the "way," the truth and the "light"

We thank you father god, that we don't have to stand in line to talk to you,

We don't have to pick up a phone and call you,

Or go no particular place or dress a certain way,

We thank you for waking us up this morning,

Starting us off in our right minds, to see this new and beautiful day,

One we've never seen before and one we will never see again,

We thank you for food on our tables and a roof over our heads,

We thank you for road mercy, and for everyone that have assemble here this morning,

We thank you for our reasonable portion of health and strength,

We thank you for making a way out of no way,

We thank you for everyone you have sent to be in our lives,

We thank you for the times we've had with the ones you have taken back,

Lead us and Guide us, to do your will,

In the mighty name of Jesus...... Amen

As Far as The East is from The West

We thank you father God,

As far as the east is from the west,

So far as you removed our transgressions from us,

You said in your word:

If we confess our sins,

You is faithful and just to forgive us our sins,

And to cleanse us from all unrighteousness,

Father God wants us to be joyful always and pray at all times,

And be thankful in all circumstances,

Help us to keep what is good,

And avoid every kind of evil,

May the God who gives us peace,

Make us holy in every way and keep our whole being,

Spirit, soul, and body free from every fault at the coming

Of our lord Jesus Christ

Amen

God Knows Our Motives

Holy Spirit,

You know our motives to why we do anything,

And by your grace we are saved,

We are more than a conqueror, through him that love us,

Father God, you are our defender and protector,

You are our God and in you we put our trust,

And may God the source of hope

Fill us with all joy and peace by the power of the Holy Spirit,

Amen

Be of Good Courage

Father; you said in your words:

Wait on the Lord and be of good courage,

And he shall strengthen our hearts,

Lord you are our help and our redeemer,

Those who wait on you shall renew their strength,

They shall mount up with wings like eagles,

They shall run and not be weary,

They shall walk and not faint,

God so loved the world that he gave his only begotten son,

That whosoever believes in him, should not perish but have everlasting life,

These many blessings and all blessings we ask in the mighty name of Jesus,

Amen

We Have Sinned

Bless us father, for we have sinned,
As your children, we have had troubles,
We have had pains, and we have had loses,
We have gone with out sleep and sometimes without food,
But, the Lord is our shepherd and we shall not want,
Help us not to be ashamed to give you honor and praise,
For it is good to sing praises to our god,
We will bless the lord at all time,
His praise shall continually be in our mouth
Amen, Amen

We Need your Love and Care

Most gracious and all powerful God,

We thank you for being our shepherd and our guide,

We will never out grow our need for your love and care,

Help us to seek you with all our hearts,

Your word is a treasure,

Priceless and beyond compare,

Let your word father God,

Saturate our minds and hearts,

Let them flow out of our mouth,

Off our lips oh so gently,

And give us the strength to deal with whatever or whoever,

We'll have to deal with in order to serve you,

In the name of Jesus we say,

Amen

Make Us Pure in Heart

Almighty God,

Help us to control our thoughts and words today,

Change us from our selfish ways and make us pure within,

Help us be a testimony for you,

Give us wisdom to know when to speak, and when not to speak,

And what to say and what not to say,

We thank you Holy Spirit for direction today

These many blessings and all blessings, we ask in your Holy Spirit

and righteousness name,

Amen

Holy Holy Holy

Holy, Holy, Holy,

Lord, God, Almighty,

Which was and is and is to come,

In your grace,

Give us unfailing courage and a firm hope,

You are worthy O Lord to receive glory and honor,

You have created all things and may the Lord himself,

Who is our source of peace,

Give us peace at all times and in every way,

And may the grace of our Lord Jesus Christ be with us all,

Amen

Our Hearts are Thankful

Father God,

Our hearts are thankful,

We thank you because you are more than enough,

Touch our sisters and brothers where they hurt the most,

Lift up their spirits,

We thank you because you did not leave us to bear our burdens alone,

We thank you because you have given us these dear ones for whom we pray,

And we are thankful for your goodness to us all,

And for your guidance in our lives,

We praise your name dear Jesus,

Who came that we might know the truth of your wonderful love,

These many blessings we ask in your name Jesus,

Amen

We Come Anxious for Nothing

Most gracious and all powerful God,

We come anxious for nothing,

But in everything we come to you in prayer,

We plead the blood over all sicknesses,

And over every situation in this life,

Father God, we ask that you listen to our hearts,

And continue to use us to do your will,

And when this old world closes in on us,

We pray that you make us go as clean as the way you created us,

We repent of our sins,

We love you, we need you,

We believe you died for us,

We receive you today in our hearts,

We thank you for everything that you have done,

Seen and unseen in the mighty name of Jesus and we say

Amen

Look Upon Us from Heaven

Lord look upon us from Heaven,
Where you live in your holiness and glory,
We are all as an unclean thing,
All our righteousness is as filthy rags,
Because of our sins, we are like leaves that,
Wither and are blown away by the wind,
But you are our father, Lord,
We are the clay and you are the potter,
You created us; be merciful to us and bless us,
Don't ever let us stray from your ways,
Amen

We Repent of Our Sins

Dear father, we repent of our sins today,

We love you, we need you, and we believe you died for us,

We receive you in our hearts right now,

Holy Spirit we need your help in our lives today,

Guide our hearts and minds,

We want our lives to tell the story of your

Goodness and your grace let your wisdom guide us and let us,

Be bold witness for you,

Use us in ways we never thought possible and give us a spirit of praise,

So that we will always give you glory, honor and praise

Amen

Be Not Conformed to this World

Father God said in his word,

Be not conformed to this world, but be,

Ye transformed by the renewing of our mind,

Then Lord, we will be able to know the will of God,

And Lord, may the God of peace provide us with every good thing,

We need in order to do his will, and may,

He through Jesus Christ; do in us what please him,

We ask you to bless our church families, our home families,

Our neighbors and friends, come into our hearts today,

Be our Lord and savior in Jesus name we pray,

Amen

Countless Blessings

Almighty God,
We offer you our humble and heartfelt thanks,
For all the countless blessings of our lives,
Your goodness cannot be measured,
We thank you for sunshine, rain, heartaches and pain,
We thank you for providing us with food and shelter,
And father God we do thank you for peace that comes to us in loving you,
You are our joy, our strength, and our help in every need,
Great is your name and greatly to be praised
Amen

Morning, Noon and Night

Father in Heaven,

You long to show us your grace and bring us into relationship with you,

Help us to choose faith in you, despite our past or present,

We thank you that,

We can come to you morning, noon or night,

If we confess our sins,

You are faithful and just to forgive us our sins,

And cleanse us from all unrighteousness,

But, if we say "we have no sin"

We deceive ourselves, and the truth in not in us,

May the God of peace,

Provide us with every good thing we need,

In order to do his will and may he,

Through Jesus Christ, do in us,

What pleases him and Christ be the glory forever and ever,

Amen

Gracious Lord

Gracious Lord,

It's not easy to swallow our pride and ask others to forgive us,

Father God gives us the strength, wisdom and grace to respond gratefully,

We thank you for your never failing presence in our lives,

And we count on your promise,

That you will never leave us nor forsake us,

Help us to grow more and more like you each day,

Yea though we walk through the valley of the shadows of death,

We will fear no evil, for you are with us, in the mighty name of Jesus

Amen

We Come as a Child

Dear heavenly father,

Whose wisdom is infinite and power without end,

We come to you as a child,

Facing the wonders and temptations of life and we thank you for its joys

and sorrows, you are our light and our salvation and we will not fear,

Because for every storm you will give us a rainbow,

And for every tear you will give us a smile,

For every prayer you will give us an answer,

These many blessings and all blessings we ask,

In your holy and righteous name,

Amen

Alpha and Omega

Alpha and Omega,
Be merciful to us and bless us,
For we are sinners,
Help us to know that the battle is not ours,
But belongs to you,
Father God we pray that you will guide,
Us and bless us with good health and habits,
And protects us from enemies and evil,
Help us to understand that true happiness in life,
Is always a gift from you,
Amen

We Pray for the Soldiers

Blessed redeemer,

We pray for the soldiers all over the world,

That's fighting for our freedom and our rights,

Go into the homes of all the peoples that is sick and suffering,

Touch each and every one with a finger of love,

Touch the ones that's being mistreated and misunderstood,

Go into the air force, army, navy, marines,

Wrap your loving arms around them and keep them safe from all hurt,

Harm and danger,

Father God, we stretch our arms out to you,

With no other help we know,

We just want to thank you for being God,

All by yourself in Jesus name,

Amen

Lord keep Us Day by Day

Everlasting father,
Bless us and keep us day by day,
Forgive us father God for most of the time,
We only give you praises if everything is going good in our lives,
Help us not forget that no matter what we are going through,
You are the same yesterday, today and forever more,
If we just hold to your hand,
You are the joy and strength of our lives,
Weeping may endure for a night,
But joy comes in the morning,
Amen

Lamb of God

Lamb of God,
Please let us say "thank you" over and over again,
For your love and blessings in our lives,
Open our eyes father God to all the wonders around us,
And keep us busy praying for your help,
And guidance in every particular of our lives,
And above all Dear Father, keep us busy doing good in your name,
Help us to forgive others when they don't want to be forgiven,
And to think always of the good in them,
No matter how upsetting they may be to us at times,
Lead us father God to always think and do the right thing,
In your name Jesus we pray and ask it all
Amen

We are Citizens of Heaven

Father above,

Help us to forget what is behind us,

And do our best, to reach for what is ahead,

We are citizens of heaven,

Eagerly waiting for our savior,

Help us father God, to always be joyful in our lives,

And to show a gentle attitude toward everyone,

Help us not to worry about anything,

But, in everything, pray and ask you, for what we need,

Father, help us to always ask with a thankful heart,

We thank you Lord, for your peace,

Which is far beyond human understanding,

These many blessings and all blessings,

We ask in the name of Jesus......Amen

Blessed not Stressed

Heavenly father,

We thank you for being our father and our guide,

We will never outgrow our need for your love and care,

We thank you father God that in every trial,

Challenge and difficulty we face,

You are behind the scenes,

Working things out, for our good,

Help us father God, to love you,

With a whole heart, soul and mind,

And give us the power, to be who you want us to be,

And to walk in your ways,

In the name of Jesus,

Amen

Strength to Face All Conditions

Heavenly father,
Give us the strength to face all conditions,
By the power that Christ gives us,
Help us not use harmful words, only helpful words,
And help us, to get rid of all bitterness and anger,
Lord, help us to be kind and tender hearted to one another,
And forgive one another as God has forgiven us,
Through Christ Jesus, we say.... Amen

We Made it Through

Most gracious and all powerful God,

Through the storms and rain,

Heartaches and pains,

We made it through,

We could have lost our minds,

But, thanks be to God,

For keeping us in our right minds,

To see this new and beautiful day,

One we've never seen before,

And one we'll never see again,

Father God, we pray for all those misjudged,

And misunderstood to have mercy,

We pray for peace, love and joy to come in our lives,

Even in those moments when we don't pray,

Keep us tender-hearted and kind,

Loyal to you father God,

In everything we do and everything we say,

Be our guiding star, this day and forevermore,

Amen

Sovereign Lord

Sovereign Lord,
Sometimes it takes a painful experience,
To make us change our ways,
Father God you allow hard things to come into our lives,
Only to make us stronger and better,
There is no respect a person with God,
All have sinned and come short of the glory of God,
Each of us should judge our own conduct,
And thank God for being the same yesterday,
Today and forever,
Amen

Show Us the Way

Almighty God,
We thank you because you have shown us the way,
The truth and the light,
Father God you have given us all things,
You said in your word:
Come to me all of you that labor and are heavy laden and I will give you rest,
You said; take my yoke upon you and learn of me,
For I am meek and lowly in heart and you shall find rest unto your souls,
We thank you; father God, if we had ten thousand tongues,
It would not be enough,
We thank you for everything,
That you have done and everything that you are still doing,
In the mighty name of Jesus,
Amen

Serving Others

Heavenly father,
We thank you, for the privilege we have to serve you,
By serving others,
And when we face sorrow, pain and hardship,
Let us not sink into self-pity,
But help us to hide ourselves in you and your word,
But help us to hold to your word,
It needs no additions or subtractions,
Help us to handle it with great care,
And to obey what it says,
We thank you lord, for your stable and unchanging hand,
And we thank you, that the battle is not ours but yours,
In the name of Jesus we ask it all,
Amen

The Most High God

The most high God,
When things look bad,
Help us to remember God is good,
Help us to realize,
When you permit trials to come into our lives,
You also provide comfort,
Help us to put ourselves in your hands and,
Ask you to make us the strong persons,
That you meant us to be,
Come, Lord, give us courage,
Fill us with your Holy Spirit,
And make us over comers,
And help us to stand fast in our faith and be brave and be strong,
For nothing is to hard for you Father God,
And whom the son set free is free indeed,
In Jesus name we say hallelujah Jesus,
Amen

Jehovah Shalom

Jehovah shalom,
Jesus said in his word:
"I am the way the truth and the life"
No one comes to the father except through me,
Lord, we are eternally thankful for the truth,
Help us to be content with what we have,
And be thankful in the place where you have put us,
So that you might be glorified through us,
Father we love you, and we need you,
And we acknowledge that we are sinners,
Father let not our hearts be troubled,
We do believe in you Lord,
And in your word,
Bless your holy name,
Hallelujah Jesus,
Amen

All Walks of Life

Blessed redeemer,
Father, we come from all walks of life,
Some say... they battling sickness,
Some say... they battling diseases,
I'm here to say; we thank you father God,
That the battle is not ours,
It belongs to you, Lord,
Help us to offer encouragement,
To those whom have lost their way,
Give us a heart, to bear others heavy burdens,
And to care about their pains and their grief,
Help us father, to take a step by reaching out to people around us,
And let our hearts reflect you Lord Jesus,
Our savior who gave up so much for us,
And may the God of hope,
Fill us with all joy and peace,
In believing that we may abound in hope,
By the power of the Holy Spirit,
In Jesus name, we say..... Amen

Live in Peace

Wonderful counselor,
We humbly bow at your feet, this morning,
Help us father seek your help in difficult times,
And help us to give an honest acknowledgement,
Of our sins and repentance to you daily Lord,
Let us know and celebrate the joyful release,
Of confessing our transgressions to you,
Father God, take away all sinful thoughts and make us pure and clean,
As we receive your guidance,
Let us become complete,
And be of good comfort and be of one mind,
And live in peace,
And may the God of love and peace,
Be with us and within us,
All the days of our lives,
We ask it all in the name of Jehovah,
Amen

God *is* Our Light

Almighty God,
You are our light, when we are in darkness,
You are a strong wind, in times of a storm,
Give us strength father God,
When uncontrollable desires, threaten our spiritual well-being,
Enable us to stand strong,
Knowing that, you are a faithful God,
And you will make a way out of no way,
We thank you, that you said in your word:
"That you will instruct us and teach us in the way we should go"
Father, we are leaning and depending on you,
To lead, guide and help us not to be stubborn,
We need you Lord Jesus every hour,
Every minute, every second of everyday,
We thank you for standing by our side,
When everyone else has left us or has let us down,
In Jesus name, we call it done... Amen

The Author and Finisher of Our Faith

Father, in the name of Jesus,

When we called on you Lord, in distress,

You answered us, and set us in a broad place,

We thank you and we give you honor and praise,

We thank you for bringing light, into the darkness of our hearts,

You said in your word:

"I am the light of the world, he who follows me,

Shall not walk in darkness,

But have the light of life",

Father God, give us wisdom, knowledge and understanding,

As we read and study your word,

We lack wisdom Lord, in many situations,

We are human,

Knowing that we are going to make mistakes,

Forgive us Lord and help us to trust in you,

And look to you, because you are,

The author and finisher of our faith,

In Jesus name,

Amen

Our Traveling Journey

Dear Lord,

On our traveling journey, it's not always easy,

Sometimes we have to cry,

We do things and say things,

We let the devil step right in,

Living a fleshly life, father God, forgive us,

For thinking that we can do life without you,

Forgive us for we know not what, we do,

We thank you Lord, for our convictions,

We thank you, for welcoming us into your family,

We thank you, for loving us no matter what we do,

Or fail to do,

For nothing shall be able to separate,

Us from the love of God,

And we shall bask in its radiance and warmth,

All the days of our lives,

In the name of Jesus,

Amen

In Our Walk with You, Lord

Heavenly father,

In our walk with you,

Some people will not understand,

They will resent the change in us,

But we know that walking with you Lord,

Means we'll be out of step with the world,

Hallelujah Jesus,

Show us how to be as acceptable of others,

As you are to us,

Help us to pursue a life style,

That demonstrates God's mercy to all,

And help us to "Love our enemies,

And do good to those who hate us,

And bless those who curse us,

And pray for those who spitefully use us"

Lord, help us to stop living in the past, it's over,

And let us be anxious for nothing, but in everything,

Come to you in prayer,

For when we come to the end of our road,

And the sun has set our souls free,

Satan will have to flee, we'll have the victory

Amen

Deceitfulness of Sin

Jesus was wounded for our transgressions,
He was bruised for our iniquities,
Lord, help our hearts not to become hardened,
From the trials of life and the deceitfulness,
Of sin, we thank you, that your word,
Contains its own kind of warning signs,
We thank you for the guidance of the Holy Spirit,
We thank you for being our Lord and savior,
Help us to be merciful just as our father,
Also is merciful and let us do unto others,
As we also want them to do unto us,
We thank you father for giving your only,
Begotten son Jesus the Christ, to die for our sins,
Help us to live a life that is pleasing to you Lord,
And we thank you for the warnings in your word,
That is intended to protect us,
In the name of Jesus,
Amen

Asking, Seeking and Knocking

Spirit of the living God,

We are asking, seeking and knocking,

We love you with all our hearts,

All our soul, and with all our strength,

And with all our mind,

Help us to love our neighbor as we love ourselves,

Father in Heaven, may your holy name be,

Honored, may your kingdom come; may your,

Will be done on earth as it is in Heaven give us today the food we need,

Forgive us the wrongs we have done,

As we forgive the wrongs others has done to us,

Do not bring us to hard testing,

But keep us safe from the evil one,

Amen

Receive the Benefits

Everlasting father,

We pray now,

That your word will be deposited in our hearts,

That we might obey it and receive its benefits,

Father God, we thank you, because,

You are there with a listening ear,

When we are hurting,

Give us humble hearts,

A love for others and spiritual power,

And give us the wisdom we need to encourage others,

In their spiritual walk and Lord,

Let our words and our ways,

Reflect the heart of God and his wisdom,

Bless the Lord, for love victorious,

Love that conquers all,

We love you, Lord,

Lift our voices in praise,

In Jesus name,

Amen

We Can Do Nothing Without You

Father... Lord of Heaven and earth,

We thank you for letting us be in this world,

But not of this world,

For it is written: "man shall not live by bread alone,

But by every word that proceed out of the mouth of God"

Father, we are leaning and depending on you,

To give us the strength to deal with,

Whatever or whoever we'll have to deal with,

In order to serve you,

We know father God that, you are all powerful,

And you said in your word:

"That you would never leave us nor forsake us"

But with you we can do all things through Christ who strengthens us,

In Jesus name.... Amen

Down Through the Years

Down through the years.. Father God,

We thank you for being so good to us,

Everything that we do for you Lord... let it be real,

When we pray... let it be real,

When we give you praise... let it be real,

We thank you father God... this morning,

Because it's a blessing to be alive,

Help us father.... to walk by faith and not by sight,

Show us your way... Lord,

We thank you... for being the head of our lives,

Without you by our side... we would not survive,

We thank you, for sitting up high and looking down low,

We know we are not worthy of anything,

But we thank you.... for loving us,

We thank you... for lifting us up,

We thank you... for letting us see one more day,

In Jesus name... Amen

Thank You

Father in Heaven,
Who knows all about us,
We just want to say "THANK YOU" it was,
Your blood that saved us look down from,
Heaven and touch our hearts,
Make us, more godly like you,
We thank you for waking us up this morning,
Starting us off in our right minds,
To see this new and beautiful day,
One we've never seen before and one, we will never see again,
We say thank you holy Jesus, we thank you for food,
On our tables, a roof over our heads,
A vehicle to drive and gas to go in it,
We thank you for our reasonable portion,
Of health and strength, we are coming,
To you as humble as we know how,
Asking for forgiveness for the sins,
We know of and the sins we don't know of,
Please forgive us for our thoughts,
They can be mighty bad sometimes,
In Jesus name,
Amen

Believe and Receive

Father in the name of Jesus,

We are not worthy lord,

To come to you,

Please come to us,

Reach you're mighty hands down and save us,

Pull us out of this stormy sea,

And enable us, to walk in the promise of your blessings,

Knowing, if we ask, you are able to do exceedingly,

Abundantly, above all that we could ever ask or think,

According to the power that works within us,

In the name of Jesus,

We receive our answer,

Not by our might,

Nor by our power,

But by your spirit,

Amen

A Heart Full of Thanks

Most gracious and all powerful God,

We come to you this morning, with a heart full of thanks,

Thanking you that,

"No weapon formed against us shall prosper"

Thanking you that you said in your word,

"Where two or three are gathered together in your name,

There you are also in the mist of them.

We come father God, thanking you,

For showing us the way, the truth and the light,

We come thanking you...

That we don't have to stand in line to talk to you,

Or pick up a phone and call you,

Or go no particular place,

Or dress no certain way,

We thank you for everybody you've sent to be in our lives,

And we thank you for the time we've had,

With the ones you have taken back,

Lead us and guide us father God to do your will,

It is in Jesus name, we say... Amen

Meditate on God's Word

Blessed savior,

When pride, arrogance and evil ways... Step in,

Help us to read and meditate on your word,

Help us to clean up our thinking,

The scripture tells us to love the Lord,

With all our heart, soul and mind,

And it says... "Not to be conformed to this world,

But to be transformed by the renewing of your mind",

Help us Father God...to think about things that are,

True, noble, pure and praise worthy,

Help our minds not to wonder to evil,

But let the wisdom of the bible,

Penetrate our thoughts and our hearts,

So that the "Lord", will preserve us from all evil,

And may he preserve our soul,

Our going out and coming in,

From this day forward and even forevermore,

In Jesus name... Amen

By Your Will and Your Power

Master and creator of Heaven, earth, sea and all that is in them,

By your will and your power, we thank you,

You have already decided what will be,

Help your followers and you servants,

To speak your message with all boldness,

Through the name of your holy servant, "Jesus",

The Lord is our shepherd and we shall not want,

Father we thank you that you are our source of hope,

You are our source of peace,

You are the God, who hears us when we pray,

Help us to focus on what means the most,

To you father God, and that's love,

Lift up our spirits,

By your strife, we are healed,

By your strife, we are delivered,

And by your strife... we are set free,

We thank you that, we are blessed and highly favored for Gods own purpose,

Use us father God, to do your will each day,

In the mighty name of Jesus the Christ

    Amen

Be Not Weary in Well Doing

Father in the name of Jesus, you said in John 5:37 that:

We have never heard your voice or seen your face,

Father, we study the scriptures,

Because we think that in them, we will find eternal life,

You said: These very scriptures speak about you,

Yet, we are not willing to come to you, in order to have life,

You said: you are not looking for human praise,

But we like to receive praises from one another,

Help us……..to try to receive praises from the one who alone is God,

Father God…..help us to set new goals in our lives,

Help us to be consistent and persistent,

In our communication with you, Lord,

And help us to realize that you have to become more important,

Father God, while we become less important,

Help us to daily seek you in prayer,

We thank you for your prophetic word that says:

"Be not weary in well doing for you shall have your promised reward",

In your name, we say hallelujah Jesus… Amen

We are Blessed

Spirit of the living God,

How we love to call your righteous and holy name,

We thank you father God, that everyday your name is the same,

In our walk of life, we've had many things to come our way,

Troubles and trials on every side,

We get trapped Father God, by material things,

We thank you Father God ...that we've been blessed,

More than words can say,

We need you Lord Jesus, morning noon and night,

We thank you for standing by us,

When everyone else have left us or let us down,

We thank you father God that we know who we are,

And we know who's we are,

We will never forget where all our help comes from,

We realize that all we have, belongs to you, father God,

And after all that we've been through,

We thank you that, we are still holding on,

Knowing, that you will never leave us nor forsake us,

And you will make a way, where there seems to be no way,

May God our father and the Lord Jesus Christ,

Give us grace and peace in the name of Jesus... Amen

We Love You and We Need You

Father God, you said in your word 2 Chronicles 7:14,
If my people which are called by my name,
Shall humble themselves and pray,
And seek my face and turn from their wicked ways,
Then will I hear from Heaven and will forget their sins,
Lord we thank you that your mercies are new every day,
Jesus we do believe that you are the son of God,
And that you are God almighty himself,
The creator of Heaven and earth,
We do believe that you are the only savior,
And that you died on the cross,
And shed your blood for us,
We repent of our sins, father God,
We love you, we need you,
We receive you as our Lord and savior... right now,
Please forgive us and save our soul,
Lift up our lives from sin and shame,
And use us now for your glory,
In the mighty name of Jesus we say
    Amen

We are A Sinner

Most gracious and all powerful God,

We are a sinner; we are a spirit being,

We have a soul and we live in a body,

We thank you father God,

That you did not give us a spirit of fear,

And we do not have to be afraid of those who kill the body,

But cannot kill the soul; rather be afraid of God,

Who can destroy both body and soul in hell,

We thank you father God,

For all the second chances that you have given us,

We thank you for never asking us to do anything,

We are not equipped to do,

We thank you father God for always providing for us,

We realize it's only by your grace and through your divine mercy,

That we have made it this far,

We thank you for all the many angels,

You have sent to lead us guide us and teach us,

Father help us to trust in you with all our hearts,

And lean not on our own understanding,

And help us...in all our ways acknowledge you,

And you shall direct our path,

We thank you father God for showing up and showing out,

In Jesus wonderful and holy name we say... Amen

THE END

May God have mercy
on your souls.
In the name of Jesus Christ our Lord,
Amen